THE RULES

Dating Journal

THE RULES

Dating Journal

ELLEN FEIN AND
SHERRIE SCHNEIDER

*Record Your Progress
from First Date to
Wedding Date!*

WARNER BOOKS

A Time Warner Company

Copyright © 1997 by Ellen Fein and Sherrie Schneider
All rights reserved.

Warner Books, Inc., 1271 Avenue of the Americas,
New York, NY 10020
Visit our Web site at http://warnerbooks.com

 A Time Warner Company

Printed in the United States of America
First Printing: October 1997
10 9 8 7 6 5 4 3 2 1

ISBN: 0-446-52314-3

Book design and composition by L&G McRee

Introduction

Are you someone who has read *The Rules* and/or *The Rules II* and thought you'd like to try dating with confidence but wondered if you would actually be able to follow all the rules? Do you start each new relationship with a vow to do The Rules this time, only to find yourself straying from The Rules path before the end of the first date? Or maybe you've been doing The Rules for a few months but you keep "slipping up" and breaking rules. Don't worry—you're not alone!

We've spoken to women at our seminars and in private consultations who are trying to do The Rules, and we've noticed that many had trouble remembering certain details, such as who initiated the first conversation with a man, what night of the week he called for a Saturday night date, and how long they stayed on the phone. Understandably, such details were sketchy in their minds because they were never that important before The Rules. So we created *The Rules Dating Journal* to encourage you to write down these details and help you date with your eyes open.

The Rules Dating Journal is a companion guide and exercise book that asks you to examine your dating history in the past as well as your present behavior so you can check your progress. Using *The Journal* will help you stick to your commitment to apply The Rules in your life on a daily and weekly basis, and it will guide you toward a relationship based on love and respect.

The Journal consists of fifty-two weekly entries that ask you to concentrate on and write about a specific topic. In addition, we have included thirteen exercises—one every four weeks—that encourage you to examine larger issues, such as your dating strengths and weaknesses and what you are looking for in a man. We have deliberately left out months and dates so you can start *The Journal* at any time, any week, and make use of a full year. You don't have to wait for January 1 to start!

Throughout *The Journal* are helpful questions about past dating experiences. If you answer them honestly, a pattern of your self-defeating behavior will emerge. Recognizing unhealthy habits in past relationships that didn't work out will motivate you to change and to stick to The Rules this time.

Take the time to remember and to write about how you behaved with boyfriends in the past, which rules you broke, and the consequences. Recording the details will help you to go forward and eventually to understand *why* you act in ways that are destructive to your purpose or demeaning to you. *The Rules* and *Rules II* are about changing your behavior, while *The Rules Dating Journal* is more analytical. Using all three is a powerful combination.

The Journal is designed to help you keep a record of relevant information on both a daily and a weekly basis. What kind of information should you record? Phone conversations and how long you stayed on the phone. What night of the week and how many days in advance a man asked you out. What happened on a date, what you like and don't like about a man, and how he behaves with others. What rules you want to break or have broken, and anything else on your mind.

Of course, we realize that you won't necessarily meet men, have dates, or receive phone calls every day of the week, so we've also included questions and exercises to think about on those "slower" days. Keep in mind that during a particular week, if you are not dating someone, you should try to practice The Rules on other people in your life, such as a male friend, girlfriend, co-worker, or relative.

The Journal helps you monitor your behavior so you don't stay in relationships that are not going anywhere. We have heard from many women who, before discovering The Rules, stayed for years in relationships with men who were clearly not right for them or not planning to marry them. They ignored or rationalized his behavior or their own actions and did not heed certain warning signs. They did not take notes, so it was easy to lie to themselves, accept less than the best, or just drift along.

Even women who know The Rules and are trying to put them into practice today admit that they don't always pay attention to important facts and actions. In essence, they hear what they want to hear and see what they want to see. They are simply not used to keeping track of the kinds of details that often determine whether or not it's a Rules relationship.

The half hour or so you spend every week recording your progress will save you time—not to mention heartache—in the long run. Here are some of the benefits of making regular entries in *The Rules Dating Journal*:

- You will be more likely to stick to The Rules if you are recording relevant details. You are more likely to incorporate The Rules into your life—not just with men, but with friends and in business relationships—if you are taking the time to write and think about them. It won't be a passing fad for you but a part of who you are.
- You will be less likely to stay in a relationship with someone who is not right for you if you are conscientious about taking notes of what you like and don't like about him, and what you are and are not willing to live with.
- You will learn more about yourself—your strengths, weaknesses, areas that need improvement—if you are writing about and comparing your past and present behavior.
- You will become a more observant and honest person if you consistently record and examine your behavior in your relationships.

If you are not in the habit of keeping a diary or remembering details, you might feel unsure about how to proceed, so here are some pointers:

- Don't write your autobiography. Writing too much will make you lose your focus. Your focus should be The Rules, not every fleeting thought you have.

- You do not have to record every word exchanged on dates, what food was ordered, and so on; stick to information relevant to The Rules. You do not even have to write full sentences; just jot down key words and phrases. You simply want to put down the facts so that you won't forget what happened, you won't ignore certain traits of his that bother you, and you won't lie to yourself or repeat behavior that doesn't work.
- Keep writing in *The Journal* even when you don't feel like it. Keep it on your night table to remind you to jot down notes when you wake up or go to sleep. *The Journal* will sort out your feelings, reinforce The Rules, and help you to understand yourself better so that you make smart decisions about men. Sometimes we just don't want to discuss our feelings with anyone, even a good friend; we're embarrassed, or we're afraid of being judged. With *The Journal*, you don't have to tell anyone—and you still get results.

Now that you understand the purpose of *The Rules Dating Journal*, get a pen and begin! Don't forget to bring *The Journal* to your next support group meeting and/or discuss what you write with a Rules-minded friend or your therapist. Sharing your Rules progress will also strengthen your commitment.

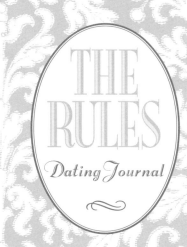

THE
RULES
Dating Journal

Week 1

$\mathcal{W}$hat led you to want to do The Rules? Did a man you wanted to marry break up with you or did you hear about other women who had success with The Rules? Write about why you are trying to do The Rules at this point in your life.

Monday

Tuesday

Wednesday

Thursday

Friday

Saturday

Sunday

In past relationships that didn't work out, did you reveal too much too soon in any way? For example, did you tell him your innermost feelings on the first or second date? List the feelings you shared prematurely so you are not tempted to spill everything on your next date.

Monday

Tuesday

Wednesday

Thursday

....

....

....

Friday

....

....

....

....

Saturday

....

....

....

....

Sunday

....

....

....

....

....

Week 3

*W*rite down which rule or rules you find hardest to do. Choose one and concentrate this week on sticking to it. Record your efforts and the results. If you are not dating someone, practice the rule on a male friend.

Monday

Tuesday

Wednesday

Thursday

....

....

....

....

Friday

....

....

....

....

Saturday

....

....

....

....

Sunday

....

....

....

....

Week 4

Try to concentrate this week on being more mysterious on dates and on the phone. Talk less, listen more, and end conversations and dates first. Record the results.

Monday

Tuesday

Wednesday

Thursday

....

....

....

Friday

....

....

....

Saturday

....

....

....

....

Sunday

....

....

....

....

....

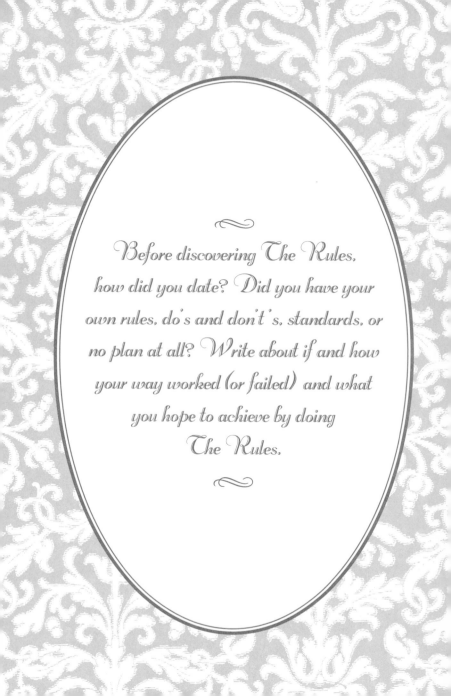

Before discovering The Rules,
how did you date? Did you have your
own rules, do's and don't's, standards, or
no plan at all? Write about if and how
your way worked (or failed) and what
you hope to achieve by doing
The Rules.

Week 5

In the past, when a man said he was unsure about his feelings for you or that he needed "space," did you try to make him talk about his feelings, tell him he was commitment-phobic, or try to convince him you were perfect for him? How would you react if this happened again?

Monday

....

....

....

....

Tuesday

....

....

....

....

Wednesday

....

....

....

....

Thursday

....

....

....

Friday

....

....

....

Saturday

....

....

....

Sunday

....

....

....

....

If you are not dating anyone, what social actions can you take this week? Write down two or three things you can do to meet men and call some girlfriends to join you—or go alone, if necessary. Make meeting a man a top priority.

Monday

Tuesday

Wednesday

Thursday

....
....
....
....

Friday

....
....
....
....

Saturday

....
....
....
....

Sunday

....
....
....
....

Week 7

$\mathscr{T}$his week, dress feminine and sexy—wear a low-cut shirt and high heels—even if you don't feel like it. Record the results. Do more men look at you or approach you? Do you feel sexier?

Monday

Tuesday

Wednesday

Thursday

....

....

....

....

Friday

....

....

....

....

Saturday

....

....

....

....

Sunday

....

....

....

....

Week 8

This week, focus on merely listening to your boyfriend's problems; try not to feel that you have to solve them for him. Write down what your advice would be, but don't tell him. This will help you to deal constructively with your feelings without bombarding him with unwanted advice.

Monday

Tuesday

Wednesday

Thursday

....

....

....

Friday

....

....

....

Saturday

....

....

....

Sunday

....

....

....

Assess your strengths and weaknesses in terms of dating. For example, your strengths could be that you look good, show up, and make a good first impression; thus you have no problem attracting men. However, your downfalls may be that you appear too eager, accept last-minute dates, or stay on the phone too long. Use this space to make a list of your dating assets and liabilities—past and present—so you know what to work on.

Week 9

Do you excuse a man's bad behavior? If the man you're dating cancels plans with you at the last minute or forgets your birthday, do you tell yourself "He's just busy" and that it's not important? This week, pay close attention to his behavior and record your observations.

Monday

Tuesday

Wednesday

Thursday

....

....

....

....

Friday

....

....

....

....

Saturday

....

....

....

....

Sunday

....

....

....

....

....

Week 10

This week, write down what behavior you simply won't put up with in a man, such as his womanizing or belittling you. If you are not dating someone, think about behavior you won't put up with in a male friend or girlfriend.

Monday

Tuesday

Wednesday

Thursday

Friday

Saturday

Sunday

Week 11

This week, make sure you're not turning yourself inside out for a man; for example, you're not adopting his interests or moving to his city in an effort to be closer to him. Write about how you may have done that in the past and how it failed. This will strengthen your commitment to be true to yourself.

Monday

Tuesday

Wednesday

Thursday

Friday

Saturday

Sunday

Week 12

If you feel you've been pursuing hobbies or interests to please him, pull back this week. Select a hobby or interest that is all your own, and record how this affects the time you spend together.

Monday

Tuesday

Wednesday

Thursday

Friday

Saturday

Sunday

In past relationships, did the man you were dating become the center of your life? For example, did you stop seeing friends or family or lose interest in your career or hobbies in order to spend more time with him? Write about your tendency to lose yourself in a relationship.

Week 13

*I*n past relationships, what kinds of things (including gifts, trips, money, cards, and letters) did you give men for their birthday, a holiday, or for no reason at all? Now that you know The Rules, do you think you gave too much? What will you give the next time?

Monday

Tuesday

Wednesday

Thursday

Friday

Saturday

Sunday

Week 14

This week, concentrate instead on giving to yourself: flowers, a professional massage, a makeover, a new tape or CD. Make a list of these necessary luxuries and keep referring to it until you have given yourself all of them.

Monday

Tuesday

Wednesday

Thursday

....
....
....

Friday

....
....
....

Saturday

....
....
....

Sunday

....
....
....
....

Week 15

This week, practice not talking to any man first. Record the results.

Monday

Tuesday

Wednesday

Thursday

....

....

....

Friday

....

....

....

Saturday

....

....

....

Sunday

....

....

....

....

Week 16

$\mathscr{M}$ake a decision not to waste time or energy thinking about men who do not call you or ask you out. Write down all that you accomplished with your newfound extra time.

Monday

Tuesday

Wednesday

Thursday

Friday

Saturday

Sunday

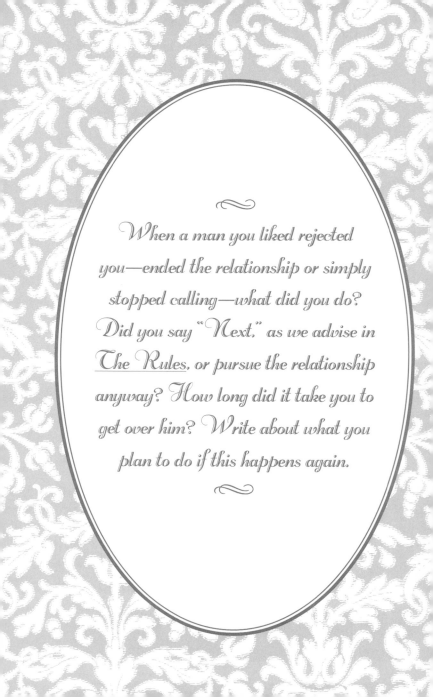

When a man you liked rejected you—ended the relationship or simply stopped calling—what did you do? Did you say "Next," as we advise in The Rules, or pursue the relationship anyway? How long did it take you to get over him? Write about what you plan to do if this happens again.

Week 17

This week, concentrate on not dating for the wrong reasons—like a fear of being alone, or your lack of faith and patience that the right man will come along. Write about fears that kept you in bad relationships in the past.

Monday

Tuesday

Wednesday

Thursday

Friday

Saturday

Sunday

Week 18

If you're angry that your boyfriend is neglecting you, do you complain to him and demand more attention? Is there a Rules way to handle this instead? Write about what rules you should follow the next time this happens.

Monday

Tuesday

Wednesday

Thursday

....

....

....

....

Friday

....

....

....

....

Saturday

....

....

....

....

....

Sunday

....

....

....

....

....

Week 19

Jot down your expectations—emotional, financial, or physical—of the man you are dating. Think about whether they are reasonable or not. This week, concentrate on managing your expectations.

Monday

Tuesday

Wednesday

Thursday

Friday

Saturday

Sunday

Week 20

This week, try to get out of any rut you may be in with the man you are dating. If things are too comfortable with your boyfriend and you feel taken for granted, shake things up a bit. If you are not dating someone, make a social change and see how this affects meeting men.

Monday

Tuesday

Wednesday

Thursday

....
....
....
....

Friday

....
....
....
....

Saturday

....
....
....
....

Sunday

....
....
....
....

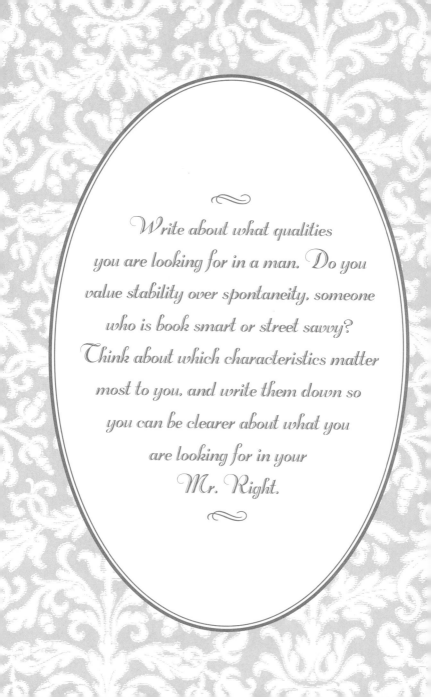

Write about what qualities
you are looking for in a man. Do you
value stability over spontaneity, someone
who is book smart or street savvy?
Think about which characteristics matter
most to you, and write them down so
you can be clearer about what you
are looking for in your
Mr. Right.

Week 21

This week, motivate yourself to end the date first and record the results. Give yourself the ammunition you need by writing about how it felt in the past when a man ended the date first, seemed bored, or the evening dragged on too long.

Monday

....

....

....

....

Tuesday

....

....

....

....

Wednesday

....

....

....

....

Thursday

Friday

Saturday

Sunday

$\mathcal{A}$re you easily hurt in relationships, not just by men but by friends, family, and co-workers who don't show more interest in you? Do you pursue these less-than-mutual relationships anyway? This week, practice making yourself less vulnerable by waiting for others to pursue you.

Monday

Tuesday

Wednesday

Thursday

Friday

Saturday

Sunday

This week, think about looking at your watch when you're on the phone with him so you don't stay on more than ten minutes. Notice how his interest seems to increase the less time you give him. Record the amount of time you spent on the phone, as well as methods for getting off first that worked.

Monday

Tuesday

Wednesday

Thursday

....

....

....

....

Friday

....

....

....

....

Saturday

....

....

....

....

Sunday

....

....

....

....

Week 24

*T*his week, think about ending a relationship with a man who says he's not the marrying kind—if you want to get married. Jot down the disadvantages of dating someone who won't commit himself to you; seeing these in black and white will help strengthen your resolve to end the relationship.

Monday

Tuesday

Wednesday

Thursday

....

....

....

Friday

....

....

....

Saturday

....

....

....

....

Sunday

....

....

....

....

Think about and record
the issues in your relationship that
could spell trouble later on. For
example, he wants to settle down in the
suburbs and you like the city; you want to
have children and he doesn't. If your attitude
is "I'll think about it _after_ we get married,"
stop and think about it now. Can you live with
these differences? Don't think love will carry
you through everything. If he proposes, you
must settle these issues before you get
married. If you are not dating
someone, apply this exercise
to a past relationship.

Week 25

This week, concentrate on compromising. This is different from pretending to have the same interests. Here you're just being a good sport, not dishonest. Try participating in some of the things he likes that you don't particularly care for—go to a scary movie, for instance—and examine the results of going along with them.

Monday

Tuesday

Wednesday

Thursday

Friday

Saturday

Sunday

Week 26

Think about what you can do to make the man in your life happy—being pleasant, light, easy to talk to, a good listener— rather than what you're hoping to get from him: attention, flowers, and so forth. Record your efforts. If you're not dating someone, practice on a friend.

Monday

Tuesday

Wednesday

Thursday

Friday

Saturday

Sunday

This week, concentrate on being a helpful and good friend, co-worker, daughter, or sister. Try to think about people in your life other than him. What effect does this have on your relationship?

Monday

Tuesday

Wednesday

Thursday

Friday

Saturday

Sunday

Week 28

*T*his week, be open to dating others if you're not dating *The One*. Motivate yourself to play the field by remembering and writing down how it felt to put all your eggs in one basket in the past.

Monday

Tuesday

Wednesday

Thursday

....
....
....

Friday

....
....
....

Saturday

....
....
....
....

Sunday

....
....
....
....
....

In past relationships, did you have a problem saying "No," setting boundaries, or doing what's in your best interests? Were you afraid that a man would lose interest if you didn't say "Yes" all the time? Are you a people-pleaser, always trying to make others happy at your own expense? Write about situations in which you should have said "No" but didn't, and ask yourself the real reasons you didn't.

Week 29

This week, think about how long you're willing to wait for the man you're dating to propose. Record any rules you could focus on if a proposal is taking longer than you'd like.

Monday

Tuesday

Wednesday

Thursday

Friday

Saturday

Sunday

Week 30

Focus this week on saying "No" and setting boundaries with a man or with people in general, even if you feel mean when you do so. Record each "No" so that you can look back later to see the effects of your actions.

Monday

Tuesday

Wednesday

Thursday

....

....

....

....

Friday

....

....

....

....

Saturday

....

....

....

....

Sunday

....

....

....

....

Week 31

Is your resolve to do The Rules weakening? Are you constantly fighting the desire to call him or ask how he feels about you? Think of what you would say to him and write it here instead. It will be another day that you didn't call him!

Monday

Tuesday

Wednesday

Thursday

....

....

....

....

Friday

....

....

....

....

Saturday

....

....

....

....

Sunday

....

....

....

....

Week 32

If you are frustrated by the delayed-gratification aspect of The Rules, write down your frustrations this week. Then write down where immediate gratification has gotten you in the past. This will strengthen your commitment to taking a long-term attitude.

Monday

Tuesday

Wednesday

Thursday

....

....

....

Friday

....

....

....

Saturday

....

....

....

....

Sunday

....

....

....

....

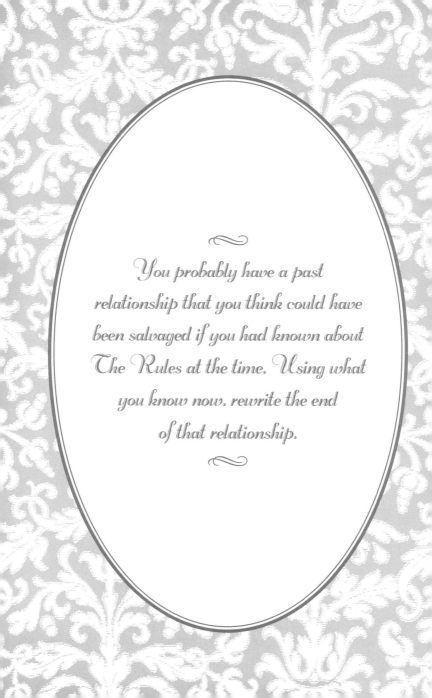

You probably have a past
relationship that you think could have
been salvaged if you had known about
The Rules at the time. Using what
you know now, rewrite the end
of that relationship.

Week 33

This week, do at least one thing other than The Rules that is not fun or easy but good for you long-term, such as giving up smoking or junk food, or sending out your résumé for a better job. Get into the habit of thinking about and taking long-term actions. It will help you do The Rules.

Monday

Tuesday

Wednesday

Thursday

....

....

....

....

Friday

....

....

....

....

Saturday

....

....

....

....

Sunday

....

....

....

....

....

*M*ake a list of ten reasons why any man would be lucky to marry you. For example, you're sexy, kind, fun to be around, smart—and, most important, now that you're doing The Rules, you're not too needy or demanding. On days when you feel low, read this list.

Monday

Tuesday

Wednesday

Thursday

Friday

Saturday

Sunday

Week 35

This week, list the ways that doing The Rules makes you more confident, poised, and independent. Positive affirmations that you're desirable will help you project that hard-to-resist Rules girl confidence.

Monday

Tuesday

Wednesday

Thursday

Friday

Saturday

Sunday

Week 36

$\mathcal{T}$*his week, make a list of what you need to make yourself more attractive—color gray hair, have your teeth bleached, lose ten pounds, stop wearing clothes that you don't look good in—and check off each item until you've done them all.*

Monday

Tuesday

Wednesday

Thursday

Friday

Saturday

Sunday

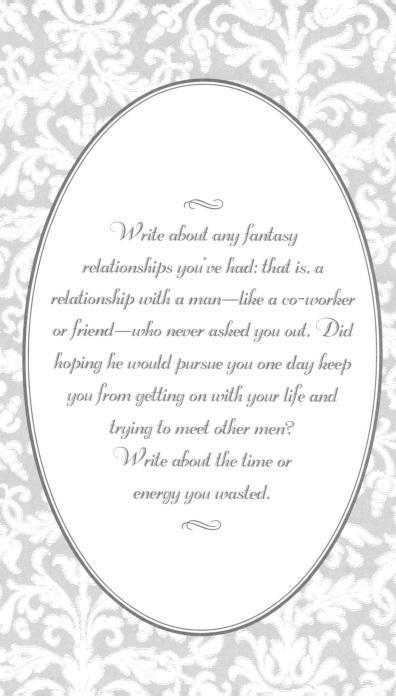

Write about any fantasy
relationships you've had: that is, a
relationship with a man—like a co-worker
or friend—who never asked you out. Did
hoping he would pursue you one day keep
you from getting on with your life and
trying to meet other men?
Write about the time or
energy you wasted.

Week 37

*I*s your whole self-worth dependent on getting a call from a man you just met on a blind date who said he'd call? Make a list of what your self-worth is *really* based on. Read this list when you feel low about him not calling—you'll feel better.

Monday

Tuesday

Wednesday

Thursday

Friday

Saturday

Sunday

Week 38

This week, work on not "coasting" on The Rules. It's easy to get a false sense of security after seeing The Rules work for the first few months, but you're not married yet, so it's more of the same! Write down your plans for resisting coasting over the next few days. It will keep you on track.

Monday

Tuesday

Wednesday

Thursday

Friday

Saturday

Sunday

Week 39

$\mathcal{T}$his week, don't try to make it easy for a man to date you—don't suggest when you're free or offer to meet him halfway. Observe the effects of this behavior and jot them down.

Monday

Tuesday

Wednesday

Thursday

Friday

Saturday

Sunday

Week 40

*I*f you feel like you can't quite relax until you *know* that the man you just started dating is going to marry you, try to find relaxation in other ways. This week, make it a point to relax through yoga, running, listening to music, or reading. List these activities and return to them when you feel stressed.

Monday

Tuesday

Wednesday

Thursday

....

....

....

....

Friday

....

....

....

....

Saturday

....

....

....

....

Sunday

....

....

....

....

In the past, did you date a man you weren't that interested in for other reasons—your mother liked him, for instance, or he made a good living, or simply because he liked you? So that you don't repeat past mistakes, write about how ulterior motives kept you in unsatisfying relationships.

Week 41

$\mathcal{T}$ry not to feel mean or guilty about doing The Rules—for instance, not calling a man back right away, not seeing him more often, or not going away with him for a week. Noting the results— his increased interest in you—will help you see that you're doing him a favor and not being mean at all.

Monday

Tuesday

Wednesday

Thursday

....
....
....

Friday

....
....
....
....

Saturday

....
....
....
....

Sunday

....
....
....
....

Week 42

Write about why having a man in your life and being married are important to you. Refer to these words when your resolve to do The Rules is faltering.

Monday

....

....

....

Tuesday

....

....

....

Wednesday

....

....

....

....

Thursday

....

....

....

....

Friday

....

....

....

....

Saturday

....

....

....

....

Sunday

....

....

....

....

....

Week 43

*A*re you a smotherer? If your boyfriend wants to celebrate New Year's with friends, do you try to make him spend it alone with you? Write about the results of smothering so that the next time you feel you must have a man "all to yourself," you have the motivation to pull back.

Monday

Tuesday

Wednesday

Thursday

Friday

Saturday

Sunday

Week 44

This week, look at any jealous streak you might have. If your boyfriend's ex-girlfriend calls or he wants to go out with the guys, do you get upset? Write down your feelings of possessiveness or insecurity, so that you don't act on these feelings in your relationships.

Monday

Tuesday

Wednesday

Thursday

Friday

Saturday

Sunday

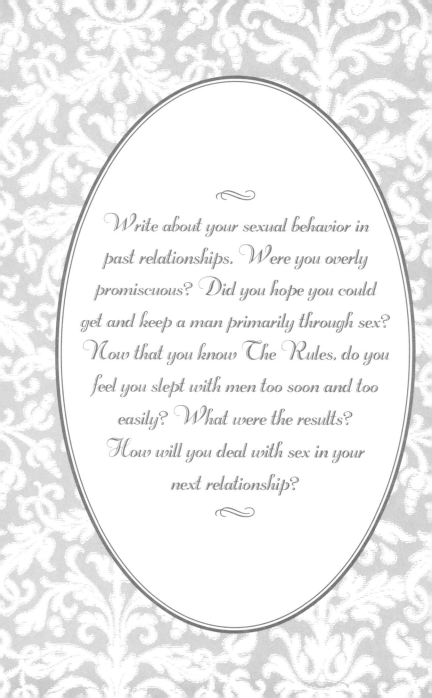

Write about your sexual behavior in past relationships. Were you overly promiscuous? Did you hope you could get and keep a man primarily through sex? Now that you know The Rules, do you feel you slept with men too soon and too easily? What were the results? How will you deal with sex in your next relationship?

After dating a man for a few months, do you start telling him how he should dress or how often he should call his parents? List any ways in which you have been controlling in past relationships and what the results were. What will you do differently next time?

Monday

Tuesday

Wednesday

Thursday

....

....

....

....

Friday

....

....

....

....

Saturday

....

....

....

....

Sunday

....

....

....

....

Week 46

*A*re you thinking about breaking a rule this week? For example, are you planning to call a man who took your number? Practice not calling him one more day, and then another and another, until the feeling passes—and it will!

Monday

Tuesday

Wednesday

Thursday

Friday

Saturday

Sunday

Week 47

This week, think about how you will feel afterward if you break a rule—especially a big one, like sleeping with a married man. Writing about the regret you will feel the next day may help you to resist temptation.

Monday

Tuesday

Wednesday

Thursday

....
....
....
....

Friday

....
....
....
....

Saturday

....
....
....
....

Sunday

....
....
....
....
....

Week 48

This week, concentrate on not preaching The Rules to anyone who is not interested. Make a list of friends and acquaintances who break rules and try to learn from their mistakes. But don't tell them what to do. They will be more impressed when they see you are dating happily or married.

Monday

Tuesday

Wednesday

Thursday

....
....
....

Friday

....
....
....
....

Saturday

....
....
....
....

Sunday

....
....
....
....
....

Is there any rule that you just don't agree with or refuse to do? For example, do you have a real problem with the concept of not talking to a man first or with waiting for him to call you? Record the results of breaking that rule in past relationships. Be sure to be honest with yourself here, because this is very difficult to do. Evaluate the results to help you decide your best Rules strategy for the future.

Week 49

This week, concentrate on not asking a man you are dating what he is planning to do with you for New Year's or Valentine's Day if he hasn't brought it up. Make a list of what you can do if he never brings it up. If you are not dating someone, write down what you will do alone or with friends for the holiday.

Monday

Tuesday

Wednesday

Thursday

....

....

....

....

Friday

....

....

....

....

Saturday

....

....

....

....

Sunday

....

....

....

....

Week 50

*W*rite about the biggest rule you broke in your last relationship. Concentrate on not breaking that rule this week. Write down the different results.

Monday

Tuesday

Wednesday

Thursday

Friday

Saturday

Sunday

Week 51

$\mathcal{T}$his week, write about the most hurtful experience you had in a relationship because you didn't do The Rules—and what you could have done differently. Writing about it will reinforce your commitment to do The Rules on the next man.

Monday

....

....

....

Tuesday

....

....

....

Wednesday

....

....

....

....

Thursday

....

....

....

Friday

....

....

....

....

Saturday

....

....

....

....

Sunday

....

....

....

....

Week 52

*A*re you placing too much importance on men because you're not fulfilled in other areas? Make a list of other areas in your life that you should be paying attention to—work, health, friendships, hobbies—so that you are less likely to break rules and you become a more well-rounded person.

Monday

Tuesday

Wednesday

Thursday

....

....

....

....

Friday

....

....

....

....

Saturday

....

....

....

....

Sunday

....

....

....

....

....

This week, describe how The Rules have changed your life—the way you date and think about and deal with men—whether you have been following them for five weeks or five months. Do you feel that The Rules are just another dating fad or a way of life for you? How committed to The Rules are you? The more you record the positive changes, the more committed you will become.